NIKKI HALEY'S JOURNEY

FROM GOVERNOR TO GLOBAL DIPLOMAT AND PRESIDENTIAL CANDIDATE

DAVID I. WOOD

DISCLAIMER

This book is a biography of Rudy Giuliani, based on publicly available information, interviews, and published works. While every effort has been made to ensure accuracy, some details may be subject to interpretation or differing accounts.

CONTENTS:

PART 1

Early Life and Family

The Randhawa Family Story (1970s)

Nikki Haley's journey begins not in the American South, but in the bustling Indian city of Amritsar. For young Ajit Singh Randhawa and his wife Raj Kaur, the 1970s are a time of transformation and promise. They are both well-educated and ambitious, and they want a better life for themselves and their children.

Ajit, a rising agricultural star, occupies a coveted job at the Punjab Agricultural University. Raj, a strong legal mind, with a law degree from the prestigious University of Delhi. A hunger for something greater stirs inside them among the hectic city life and rising jobs.

The winds of opportunity sweep westward, whispering of a country where aspirations may take flight and hard effort pays well. America, the ray of hope, calls. Ajit and Raj leave behind their family and friends in 1964, with resolve in their hearts and luggage full with ambitions. They travel to Canada because of the promise of educational prospects for Ajit. He receives his Ph.D. from the University of British Columbia with grit and persistence, paving the road for their American dream.

The Randhawas arrive in South Carolina five years later, in 1969, a sharp contrast to the busy streets of Amritsar. They settle in Bamberg, a peaceful, largely white village in the heart of the American South. They are faced with the obstacles of navigating a new culture and starting again.

Ajit gets a job teaching at Voorhees College, a historically black college, while Raj gets her master's degree in education and starts teaching in the public-school system. They are pioneers in their own right, laying the groundwork for future Indian immigrants in their adoptive town.

Their lives are blessed in 1972 with the birth of their first and only child, a girl named Nimrata Nikki Randhawa. Nikki's Bamberg upbringing is a mosaic of two separate cultures. Her parents immerse her in their Punjabi history at home, infusing the house with the smells of spices and the colorful sounds of Punjabi. She navigates the world of Southern America at school and in the neighborhood, encountering subtle shades of discrimination and forming connections with youngsters from other origins.

Nikki thrives despite the obstacles. She is a bright, inquisitive youngster who excels in her schoolwork and has a passion for leadership. Her parents, who are always supportive, develop her abilities and teach in her the principles of hard work, tenacity, and steadfast faith. Nikki's upbringing, a unique combination of Sikh ideals and American aspirations, sets the foundation of her future, developing her into the strong, determined woman she would become.

The Randhawa family tale is about more than simply overcoming obstacles and reaching success. It exemplifies the lasting strength of family, the relentless pursuit of aspirations, and the bravery to welcome new beginnings. The roots of Nikki Haley's journey may be traced back to the sun-drenched streets of Amritsar and the quiet resilience of a little town in South Carolina, as she enters the international stage, carrying the flame of her immigrant parents' struggles and unflinching belief.

Growing Up in Bamberg

Bamberg, South Carolina, in the 1970s and 1980s, was a world different from Amritsar's busy streets. Life in this mostly white Southern town, nestled among rolling hills and cotton farms, was a sharp contrast to the vivid tapestry of Nikki's Indian ancestry. Nonetheless, Nikki's youth grew inside the confines of Bamberg, shaped by a distinct combination of immigrant ideals and southern charm.

Nikki's house was a cultural melting pot. The lyrical rhythm of Punjabi mingled with the drawl of Southern accents in the air. On the one hand, Raj and Ajit kept their Indian origins alive by cooking curries and samosas, telling folktales about valiant monarchs and wise saints, and celebrating bright holidays like Diwali with colorful rangoli and traditional sweets. Nikki, on the other hand, ventured out into the world, attending church picnics, learning line dancing at county fairs, and soaking in the warmth of Southern hospitality.

Life was not without its difficulties. Trying to navigate two diverse cultures provided its own set of challenges. Nikki felt the pain of subtle bias at school, when she encountered peers who couldn't pronounce her name or murmured about her "different" lunches. She struggled at home to reconcile her American identity with her parents' expectations. Nonetheless, Nikki developed a unique ability to bridge the gaps inside this dualism. She quickly learned to code-switch, changing her vocabulary and demeanor to the situation. This chameleon-like ability, forged in the fires of her youth, would eventually become one of her distinguishing characteristics, helping her to connect with varied audiences and negotiate difficult political terrain.

Despite the difficulties, Nikki's parents remained her rock. They instilled in her principles that cut across cultures: a strong work ethic, a firm belief in education, and the significance of giving back to the community. Nikki observed firsthand the power of service and selflessness, from Ajit's passion to teaching to Raj's commitment to social justice. These ideals became invisible threads woven into her essence, directing her decisions and defining her future course.

Nikki's independence was also fostered by Bamberg. She acquired a strong sense of self-belief as a result of her parents' encouragement to question, investigate, and challenge the current quo. She was involved in student government, succeeded academically, and even defied the school clothing policy with her love of colorful saris. Nikki learnt to speak her mind and forge her own path growing up in a tiny town with a broad worldview, skills that would catapult her into the arena of public service.

Bamberg may have been a sleepy corner of the American South, but it was a fruitful environment for Nikki's growth. She traversed two cultures, bridged gaps, and accepted a diversified identity within its constraints. She discovered the importance of hard labor, the strength of community, and the fortitude to speak up for what she believed in. These teachings, inscribed in her early memories, would serve as an invisible compass, taking her from the cotton fields of Bamberg to the halls of power, making an everlasting influence on the American political scene.

Ambition and Education

Nikki Haley grew up in Bamberg, South Carolina, where she developed a strong work ethic, cultural literacy, and a growing ambition. As she entered her adolescence, the seeds of intellectual curiosity and professional ambition began to blossom, eventually taking her to the hallowed halls of Clemson University and, eventually, the vibrant world of corporate America.

Nikki, then 17, arrived on the Clemson campus in 1989, a colorful center of orange and purple tucked among South Carolina's undulating hills. Nikki grew as she was immersed in a varied student population and a tough academic atmosphere. She was drawn to the discipline and logic of accounting and developed her leadership abilities via extracurricular activities such as the National

Association of Intercollegiate Athletics (NAIA) student-athlete advisory council.

Clemson not only academically pushed Nikki, but also enlarged her outlook. She spent a semester in India through the university's foreign exchange program, immersing herself in her ancestral origins and obtaining vital intercultural perspectives. This experience honed her ability to negotiate multiple ideas and cultures, which she would need in her future political career.

Nikki's time at Clemson was not all about academics and international travel. She acquired a love for dancing, taking part in the Clemson University dancing Marathon and even choreographing routines for her classmates. Her participation in extracurricular activities demonstrated her ability to connect with individuals from all backgrounds as well as her desire to thrive outside of the limits of a textbook.

Nikki graduated in 1994 with a Bachelor of Science degree in accounting and a heart full of passion. Nikki was ready to answer the call of the world beyond Clemson.

Nikki's early post-graduate years were filled with a flurry of professional endeavors. She secured a desirable position at Lexington County's tax department, where she gained important expertise in the complexities of public finance. But the corporate world quickly called, allowing Nikki the chance to use her abilities and desire on a wider scale.

As a financial analyst, she joined the global logistics behemoth Electronic Data Systems (EDS) in 1995. Nikki thrived here, her innate talent for mathematics and her unwavering work ethic driving her through the ranks. She worked on difficult financial initiatives, learned about international business, and refined her capacity to flourish in a fast-paced, multicultural atmosphere.

Was not afraid to tear down barriers inside EDS. She experienced subtle prejudices and cultural obstacles as one of the few women and minorities in a male-dominated sector. Her strength and resolve, however, shined through. Her expertise and work ethic gained her colleagues' respect, demonstrating her capacity to bridge cultural barriers and achieve agreement in even the most difficult circumstances.

Nikki's stint at EDS was defined by the assignment of establishing a new financial system in India. This endeavor took her out of her comfort zone, asking her to manage cultural nuances as well as practical challenges. Nikki, on the other hand, rose to the occasion, effectively implementing the system and demonstrating her capacity to flourish in foreign environment.

Her aspirations evolved as she ascended the corporate ladder at EDS. The joy of crunching figures was increasingly overshadowed by a desire for a more influential function, one that directly influenced the lives of people. This ambition eventually drove her to investigate the realm of politics, a route that would change the course of her life dramatically.

Nikki's experience in the corporate sector shaped her into a savvy entrepreneur, effective negotiator, and culturally aware leader. The skills she gained throughout those years about financial savvy, tenacity, and negotiating varied cultures would serve as stepping stones to her political career.

As we leave Nikki at the crossroads of ambition and opportunity, a question lingers: will she continue her stratospheric climb in the corporate world, or will she respond to the call of a different sort of leadership, one that offers challenges and rewards that go well beyond the bottom line? Stay tuned for the next instalment of Nikki's narrative, in which she takes a leap of faith into the unpredictable realm of South Carolina politics, abandoning the predictability of spreadsheets for the exhilaration of establishing her own political destiny.

Entering Politics and the Rise of a Young Conservative

Nikki Haley's decision to enter politics was the result of a growing desire to make a difference and a flame kindled by a local injustice. A close friend, a successful Indian-American businesswoman, was discriminated against by a county official in 2004. Witnessing the act and its aftermath sparked Nikki's outrage, sparking a desire to use her voice to challenge discrimination and fight for justice.

Well aware that entering politics would be a drastic departure from the security of business life. Nonetheless, she chose to run for a position in the South Carolina House of Representatives, fueled by her newfound passion and backed by her family. The campaign was a challenging learning experience. Nikki, who was used to giving boardroom speeches, had to learn the art of town hall meetings and door-to-door talks. She negotiated the complexities of grassroots campaigning, interacting with individuals from all political stripes and learning to convert her business experience into a vernacular that connected with the audience.

In 2004, Nikki Haley, a young Indian-American woman with a business background, stood out in South Carolina politics, which was controlled by white men. Her outsider status, on the other hand, proved to be a benefit. She campaigned on a platform of economic discipline, school reform, and social justice, promising people tired of the status quo a new viewpoint.

Nikki's campaign was powered by her unwavering enthusiasm and genuine participation. She communicated with voters rather than to them, listening to their problems and exhibiting a thorough awareness of their difficulties. Her ability to interact with various groups was critical to her success, which made her the first person of Indian heritage and the youngest female minority member ever elected to South Carolina's House of Representatives.

Republican Party Rising Star

Nikki wasted no time in demonstrating her worth after being elected. She swiftly rose through the Republican ranks, garnering recognition for her sharp intelligence, strong work ethic, and steadfast dedication to her constituency. She championed significant legislation, took on sensitive subjects like as welfare reform, and emerged as a strong advocate for education and economic growth.

The rise Nikki, however, was not without its difficulties. She confronted both subtle and overt prejudices as a conservative lady of color in a largely white party. But Nikki faced these problems full on, never being afraid to speak up or stand up for what she believed in. Her toughness and perseverance only served to strengthen her image as a formidable opponent.

By 2010, Nikki Haley had established herself as a rising political figure in South Carolina. Her hard ethic, intellect, and charisma had earned her great acclaim, propelling her to a larger platform. Nikki set her eyes on the highest post in the state, the governorship, with the backing of her party and a growing following of supporters.

The 2010 gubernatorial election marked a watershed point in Nikki's career. She had a seasoned opponent in the Democratic incumbent, but people responded positively to her energy, excitement, and message of change. Nikki Haley, 38, made history by becoming South Carolina's first female and minority governor, smashing multiple glass ceilings and demonstrating that desire combined with hard effort can genuinely lead to great results.

As we depart Nikki is on the verge of becoming governor, and the future spreads out before her, loaded with possibilities. The young lady who discovered her voice in the struggle against injustice is now poised to govern a state, eager to leave her imprint on the political scene and inspire a new generation of leaders. Stay tuned as we enter the next chapter of her journey, in which Nikki Haley faces governance obstacles, navigates the complicated world of national politics, and emerges as a significant player on the Republican stage, with her eyes set even higher.

PART 2

Political Career in South Carolina

Nikki Haley's 2004 year wasn't simply about turning 32 or receiving another business rise. It was a year of personal awakening, a watershed moment in which the light of civic involvement shone brilliantly, revealing a route toward a career characterized by public service and political ambition. This route began in the furnace of the South Carolina State House contest, a hard experience that provided the framework for a remarkable change from businesswoman to lawmaker.

While Haley's career advancement had been great, something deeper was stirring inside her. Witnessing a close friend, an Indian-American businesswoman, being treated unfairly by a local official sparked a sense of unfairness that refused to go away. The encounter served as a catalyst, pushing her to confront the realities of prejudice and driving her determination to fight for fairness and equality. This personal experience, along with a growing frustration with the established quo, pushed Haley into a world far distant from boardrooms and financial projections: the dark, thrilling world of politics.

Her entry into politics was a risky move. The realm of campaign rallies and town hall meetings was a parallel planet to the regimented limitations of business discussions. Nonetheless, she embraced this new endeavor with the same determination and commitment that had distinguished her professional career. She engaged herself in the complexities of grassroots campaigning, learning to negotiate the delicate dance of voter engagement, understanding local problems, and translating her corporate experience into a language that connected with voters.

Haley's 2004 campaign for the South Carolina House of Representatives was everything but conventional. Her candidacy was a one-of-a-kind outlier. She was a young Indian-American woman in a field dominated by white, male veterans. Every step of the way, she had to battle stereotypes and preconceived beliefs.

Haley, on the other hand, converted these seemingly insurmountable difficulties into strengths. Her outsider status became a refreshing influence, providing people disillusioned with traditional politicians with a new perspective. Her youth was viewed as a sign of vitality and transformation, and her economic acumen fostered trust in her capacity to deal with complicated challenges.

Campaign plan included more than just slogans and rallies. It was all about true participation. She knocked on voters' doors, listened to their issues, and displayed empathy for their plight. She talked not to, but with, the voters, weaving real stories into her agenda, which emphasized economic prudence, school reform, and social justice.

This tactic was critical in breaking down barriers and gaining support across party lines. Resonating with her message of justice and opportunity, black voters banded together with conservative white voters who associated with her budgetary discipline and strong work ethic. This diversified coalition pushed Haley to a hard-fought win, making her the first woman of Indian origin and the youngest female minority member in South Carolina House of Representatives history.

From Candidate to Lawmaker

Entering the state house was not a victory lap, but rather the start of a difficult path. Haley rapidly removed her campaigning skin and assumed the mantle of a lawmaker. She engaged herself in the complexities of government, serving on committees, researching legislation, and actively engaging in legislative discussions.

Her acute intelligence, along with her ability to swiftly understand difficult subjects, gained her respect on all sides of the aisle. She was an outspoken advocate for budgetary prudence and championed crucial legislation on school reform. She also supported initiatives aimed at luring businesses and generating employment. Her work ethic was famous, and she was a continuous presence in committee meetings and on the House floor.

Her ascension, however, was not without its difficulties. She encountered subtle and not-so-subtle discrimination and bias as a young, progressive Republican woman in a conservative, male-dominated setting. Nonetheless, Haley, true to her, faced these problems straight on. She was never afraid to speak her mind or fight for what she believed in, displaying a steely grit and strong independence that would become her trademark.

Nikki Haley has progressed from a potential novice to a seasoned politician and rising figure within the Republican Party by 2010. Her work ethic, intellect, and unshakable dedication to her constituency had won her considerable acclaim. She was known for her bipartisanship, reaching across the aisle to find common ground while remaining loyal to her conservative values.

More significantly, she had an extraordinary capacity to connect with voters, winning their confidence and respect by her genuineness, empathy, and unrelenting commitment to public service. This combination of attributes put her in a strong position, laying the framework for the next, more difficult stage in her political career: the governor's seat, the ultimate prize in South Carolina politics.

Haley's campaign strategy, established during her time in the state legislature, stayed consistent: real participation. She traveled the state diligently, holding town halls, attending neighborhood events, and drinking coffee with folks in their homes. She addressed citizens' issues with honesty and empathy, avoiding political jargon.

Many South Carolinians, tired of economic stagnation and dissatisfaction with the existing quo, want change. Haley tapped on this feeling, exuding a powerful picture of energy and purpose. She pledged to shake things up by bringing new viewpoints and creative solutions to the state's challenges. This message resonated with voters of all demographics, garnering support from suburban housewives, white conservatives, and even some African Americans who regarded her as a departure from the old political landscape.

On the night of the 2010 election, history was created. Nikki Haley, 38, became South Carolina's first female governor and first governor of Indian origin. Her win was a credit to her unshakable work ethic, ability to connect with voters, and faith in her vision for the state. It also sent shockwaves through the national political scene, heralding the emergence of a new generation of diverse Republican leaders willing to break the pattern.

Nikki Haley stood not just as the newly elected leader of South Carolina, but also as a symbol of optimism for millions as the first gavel pounded, signalling the start of her governor tenure. She demonstrated that political success was not restricted to professional politicians or established dynasties. Anyone, regardless of color, gender, or origin, with hard effort, a compelling message, and a real desire to serve, may do it.

State Representative to Minority Leader

Nikki Haley's election to the South Carolina State House in 2004 was more than just a personal success; it signalled the start of a strategic rise inside the Republican Party. Haley wasn't happy to merely be a vociferous politician in the hallways of the legislature; she set her eyes on establishing a power base, strengthening her influence, and eventually securing the coveted post of Minority Leader.

The two years in the State House were a blur of learning and adjusting. She immersed herself in legislative procedures, navigating committee sessions, learning the art of bargaining, and creating cross-partisan partnerships. While she advocated for budgetary discipline and social conservatism, she also shown pragmatism by working with Democrats on subjects like as education reform and infrastructure development. This determination to find common ground garnered her respect from colleagues on both sides of the aisle, paving the way for future leadership positions.

Haley valued connection development over policy and procedure. She diligently sought out Republican Party mentors, soaking up their knowledge and navigating the often-muddy waters of political maneuvering. She formed relationships with other young Republicans, many of whom identified in her a kindred spirit - a new face with daring ideas and a steadfast dedication to change.

More significantly, Haley recognized the need of interacting with varied constituencies. She sought out to the state's burgeoning Indian-American minority, bridging the cultural divide between her heritage and the mainstream Republican base. She was involved in African-American communities, listening to their issues and fighting for legislation that met their needs. This inclusive attitude aided her in broadening her political footprint and cultivating a devoted following outside of the conventional Republican demographic.

Haley's hard work and savvy relationships yielded immediate results. She was elected House Majority Whip in 2008, just four years after joining the State House, becoming the first woman and first person of color to hold the office. This dramatic ascent cemented her credentials as a rising star inside the Republican Party, demonstrating her leadership abilities, ability to rouse the troops, and ability to navigate the intricate processes of legislative politics.

Her role as Whip extended beyond internal party management. She became an important participant in crafting the legislative agenda, working closely with Republican leadership to ensure major bill approval while keeping her fellow House Republicans together and disciplined. This taste of leadership spurred her desire even more, and she set her eyes on the ultimate prize in the House: the coveted job of Minority Leader.

With the winds of political revolution flowing across South Carolina in 2010, Haley took her most daring move yet. She campaigned against Bobby Harrell, the seasoned Republican incumbent, for the office of Minority Leader. The state political environment was rocked by this decision. Haley's candidacy as a young woman of color against a white, established figure was viewed as a risk, a potential upset that may transform the state's political landscape.

Haley's campaign was founded on the same tenets that had carried her to previous success: hard work, inclusion, and a message of change. She vowed to energize the Republican Party, broaden its appeal, and present a more united front against the Democratic majority. She relentlessly campaigned around the state, meeting with fellow Republicans and passionately arguing for her vision of stronger, more diverse leadership.

Haley beat Harrell in a surprising upset, becoming the first woman and first person of color to be elected Minority Leader in the South Carolina House of Representatives. This momentous triumph cemented her place on the national scene as a rising star, demonstrating that drive, combined with effective outreach and a compelling message, can overcome entrenched hierarchies and smash glass ceilings.

She had an uphill struggle as Minority Leader. Her capacity to actively influence legislation was restricted due to the Democrats' large majority. Nonetheless, she demonstrated skill in using her political capital. She effectively opposed the Democratic agenda, holding them accountable for their policies and advocating for the Republican vision. More significantly, she utilized her leadership to further unify the Republican Party, bringing together disparate elements and forming a coherent force ahead of the 2010 gubernatorial elections.

As Minority Leader, Haley was a masterpiece in political strategy and coalition building. She demonstrated that leadership was more than simply a title; it was about vision, perseverance, and the capacity to inspire and unify people. She had already established herself as a powerful force in South Carolina politics by the time she set her sights on the governor's house in 2010, a leader with a proven track record and a passionate vision for her state's future.

The Gubernatorial Election

Nikki Haley's rapid climb through the ranks of South Carolina politics culminated in her bold run for governor in 2010. This was more than a campaign; it was a seismic upheaval in the state's political landscape, a David-and-Goliath war that defied convention and smashed glass ceilings.

Taking against the Democratic incumbent, Steve Colbert, was no easy task. Colbert was a seasoned politician who was well-liked by his supporters, whereas Haley, despite her accomplishments as State Representative and Minority Leader, remained an outsider, a young woman of color bucking the mostly white, male establishment.

Haley, on the other hand, was not afraid of a challenge. She set out on a trip that would rewrite South Carolina's political history, armed with a bold vision for the state's future and a campaign strategy fuelled by inclusion and enthusiasm.

She has declined to be labelled as a "minority candidate." While recognizing her historic campaign, she focused on topics that were important to all voters, including the suffering economy, job creation, and education reform. She ran on a fiscally responsible platform, vowing to simplify government, decrease taxes, and bring businesses to the state. Her message resonated with a wide electorate, crossing party lines and appealing to independents and disillusioned Democrats alike.

Campaign approach was mainly reliant on actual participation. She crisscrossed the state, hosting town halls, visiting community events, and meeting people in person. Her ability to engage with people on a human level, speak their language, and address their issues with empathy and honesty struck a chord, especially with minority and rural groups that felt ignored by the political elite.

South Carolina, still reeling from the effects of the economic downturn and disillusioned with the existing quo, yearned for new leadership. Haley tapped into this sentiment by exuding enthusiasm and purpose. She pledged to shake things up, to bring fresh ideas and a strong work ethic to the governor's mansion. This message resonated with people from all demographics, including suburban housewives, disillusioned Democrats, and African Americans who regarded her as a departure from the typical political mold.

Despite the fact that she was up against a well-funded incumbent and established political interests, Haley's campaign gathered traction. Her unwavering energy, captivating demeanor, and message of change resonated with voters, eroding Colbert's support and garnering a wide coalition of followers.

On the night of the 2010 election, history was made. Nikki Haley, 38, became South Carolina's first female governor and first governor of Indian origin. Her triumph sent shockwaves around the country, demonstrating her persistence, ability to connect with voters, and unshakeable conviction in her vision for the state.

Haley's victory was more than simply a personal success; it signaled the beginning of a new era in South Carolina politics. It broke down racial and gender boundaries, demonstrating that skill, hard effort, and a compelling message could propel anybody, regardless of background, to the state's highest office. It also functioned as a national watershed moment, highlighting the advent of a diverse new generation of Republican leaders eager to reshape the landscape.

As the first gavel sounded, signaling the start of her governor term, Haley realized the hard job had just begun. She took on a state that had been devastated by the crisis, was highly split on social issues, and was dealing with long-standing problems. Haley was ready to face these difficulties with the same tenacity that propelled her to victory, ushering South Carolina into a new period of economic prosperity, social reform, and national acclaim.

Governor Haley

Nikki Haley's election to the governorship in 2010 represented a new chapter not just in her personal life, but also in the history of South Carolina. With a clear mandate for change, Haley focused on rebuilding the state's economy and revamping the education system, two pillars she saw as critical to South Carolina's future.

South Carolina, which had been severely harmed by the crisis, sorely needed an economic makeover. Haley recognized the importance of this need and made job development a centerpiece of her administration. She promoted pro-business measures, such as lowering taxes and regulations, in order to attract new businesses and investments. cutting the business income tax, cutting unemployment insurance fees, and expediting licensing processes were among the measures implemented.

Her efforts were rewarded. Major firms began to set up shop in South Carolina, enticed by the improving economic climate. Boeing opened a manufacturing factory, Volvo Cars announced a billion-dollar manufacturing plant, and Google opened a data center, creating thousands of employments and pouring much-needed money into the state economy.

However, Haley's strategy was not primarily aimed at luring huge firms. She understood the significance of encouraging small enterprises and entrepreneurship. She enacted policies such as the "Main Street Jobs Act," which gave tax cuts and subsidies to small companies, and the "Entrepreneur Friendly State Initiative," which intended to simplify rules and assist new entrepreneurs.

These initiatives, together with her emphasis on workforce development and job training programs, produced notable outcomes. South Carolina's unemployment rate fell gradually from 10.9% when Haley assumed office to 4.1% at the end of her first term. This economic recovery not only improved the lives of many South Carolinians, but it also enhanced the state's national standing, drawing further investment and possibilities.

Haley was a great believer in education as the foundation of social mobility and economic growth. As a result, she launched a series of bold changes aimed at enhancing the state's public education system. She advocated for measures such as school choice programs, which provide parents additional alternatives for their children's education. She also put in place teacher assessment procedures and performance-based financing, with the goal of incentivizing success and holding schools accountable.

While some welcomed Haley's education reforms for emphasizing responsibility and individual choice, others believed they deepened systemic disparities and harmed public education. Some of her plans, such as a voucher scheme to provide low-income families more access to private schools, were met with vehement criticism from teachers' unions and education activists.

Despite the difficulties, Haley remained steadfast in her goal of a changed school system. She prioritized early childhood education programs, boosted money for technical and vocational training, and put in place strategies to attract and retain skilled teachers. Her initiatives resulted in higher standardized test scores and graduation rates, demonstrating the potential of her changes to help kids throughout the state.

Governor Haley's accomplishments in addressing South Carolina's economic and educational difficulties have not gone ignored. Her daring changes, along with her charming personality and telegenic attitude, catapulted her to national prominence. She rose to prominence in the Republican Party, hailed for her fiscal conservatism, emphasis on job development, and willingness to confront difficult subjects.

Haley's national image grew as a result of her candor on a variety of political topics. She became a prominent opponent of President Obama's policies, particularly those concerning healthcare and foreign policy, and her conservative views resonated with a Republican base that was becoming weary of weak leadership.

However, Haley's rise to national fame was not without stumbling blocks. Her stances on certain social issues, such as her opposition to same-sex marriage, drew condemnation from liberals. Furthermore, her handling of problems such as the Confederate flag controversy led to charges of catering to the state's conservative constituency.

Despite these difficulties, Haley's star shone brightly on the national stage. She vigorously campaigned for Republican candidates around the country, becoming a popular speaker at conferences and conventions, and her name began to appear in speculations about prospective presidential candidates in the 2018 race.

PART 3

Ambassador to the United Nations.

Haley's nomination sparked an outpouring of support. Critics, both inside and outside the UN, cited her lack of foreign policy expertise and aggressive attitudes on Iran and Israel. There were concerns that she would further isolate the US and intensify current tensions within the international organization. Some Republicans, on the other hand, applauded Haley's selection, seeing her as a fiery and outspoken defender for American interests capable of shaking up the UN's alleged anti-American tilt.

Despite the outcry, Haley accepted the challenge. She put up a team of seasoned diplomats and foreign policy specialists to help bridge the gap between her relative inexperience and the complicated demands of the UN job. Her strategy combined a practical awareness of American interests with a willingness to address perceived injustices and inefficiencies inside the organization.

Haley's term was distinguished by a refreshingly direct attitude. She did not hold back in condemning the UN's human rights record, notably its purported anti-Israel bias. She advocated for organizational improvements, seeking greater openness and responsibility. Her outspoken support for Israel and strong opposition to Iran's nuclear program resonated with many conservatives, strengthening her reputation as a global champion of American principles.

However, Haley's record at the UN was not characterized entirely by conflict. She also looked for possibilities for collaboration, collaborating with allies on topics like as North Korea's nuclear aspirations and the humanitarian crises in Syria and Yemen. She was involved in developing countries, emphasizing the significance of economic growth and good governance in creating peace and security.

Nikki Haley and the Iranian Labyrinth

From 2017 to 2018, Nikki Haley served as the United States' Ambassador to the United Nations, where she waged a relentless war against Iran, whom she called America's "greatest adversary." Her approach, which was a sharp contrast to the Obama administration's engagement plan, sparked a whirlwind of controversy, leaving behind a complicated legacy of accomplishments, problems, and persistent ambiguity.

Haley stated unequivocally her opposition to the Joint Comprehensive Plan of Action (JCPOA), Iran's 2015 nuclear deal. She slammed its perceived faults, claiming that it failed to adequately curb Iran's nuclear goals and encouraged the regime's backing for terrorism and Middle Eastern destabilization.

Her resistance was more than simply bluster. She led a multi-pronged plan to demolish the JCPOA and put maximum pressure on Iran. Her actions included the following:

Lobbying for harsher sanctions: Haley tirelessly rallied allies within the UN Security Council to impose new sanctions on Iran's ballistic missile program and human rights abuses. Due to Russian and Chinese opposition, her achievement was limited, with only minor increases in sanctions implemented.

Using procedural tactics: Haley was not afraid to use procedural procedures to postpone voting on Iranian measures that suited the government. This enraged Tehran and annoyed other diplomats, but it demonstrated her determination and clever use of the United Nations platform.

Publicly exposing Iranian misdeeds: Haley vigorously utilized her UN platform to highlight Iran's breaches of the JCPOA and its malicious operations throughout the Middle East. Her angry statements drew media attention and popular sympathy for her viewpoint in the United States, but they also heightened tensions with Iran.

Reactions and Consequences

Haley's actions elicited a barrage of reactions:

Iran: Tehran condemned Haley's actions as unfriendly and unhelpful, accusing her of warmongering and weakening regional stability. They sensed the mounting strain but remained stubborn, demonstrating Haley's forceful approach's shortcomings.

US Allies: Haley's worries on Iran's nuclear program and regional activities were shared by certain European allies, but their opinions on the JCPOA and her aggressive approach diverged significantly. Several others voiced concern about alienating Iran and stymieing diplomatic attempts, causing conflict in the international community.

Domestic Politics in the United States: Within the United States, Haley's attitude resonated with many Republicans who regarded her as a fearless protector of American interests. Democrats and some foreign policy experts, on the other hand, chastised her for inflaming tensions, impeding diplomacy, and potentially pushing the US closer to war with Iran.

Haley's views on Iran has shifted over her tenure. While her commitment to undermining the JCPOA remained unequivocal, she shown some flexibility in meeting with other UN member states to address particular concerns about Iran's ballistic missile program and regional impact. This, however little, movement suggested a readiness to seek additional sources of pressure other than open condemnation.

President Trump removed the US from the JCPOA in 2018, putting the pact in peril as a result of Haley's unrelenting criticisms. While Haley declared this a triumph, the long-term implications are still being debated. Iran has restarted uranium enrichment, increasing concerns about a nuclear weapons race. Regional tensions have risen, with proxy wars erupting and the prospect of direct confrontation increasing. Allies questioned the US's unilateral move and commitment to multilateralism, further dividing the international community.

Haley's impact on US-Iran policy is still being written. Her supporters applaud her for boosting international awareness of Iran's nuclear program and putting pressure on the regime. They praise her with bolstering US aggressiveness and pushing back against Iranian aggression.

Detractors, on the other hand, claim that her combative strategy backfired, alienating friends, stifling negotiation, and eventually driving Iran closer to nuclearization. They warn of rising regional insecurity and geopolitical threats as a result of her initiatives.

Finally, the long-term consequences of Haley's Iran policy are unknown. The future of Iran's nuclear program, the trajectory of US-Iran relations, and the broader geopolitical landscape will determine whether she is remembered as a champion of American interests who boldly confronted a dangerous adversary or as a catalyst for instability and diplomatic impasse.

UN Reform and Modernization

With its complex bureaucracy, competing interests, and historical baggage, the United Nations has long been a target for reform suggestions. Calls for more openness, accountability, and efficiency are common, typically coming from member states dissatisfied with the organization's slowness and alleged bias.

Haley, equipped with her governorship's pragmatism and a fair dose of American scepticism, met the task front on. She listed five critical areas in need of reform:

Financial accountability: Haley slammed the United Nations' huge budget and dubious spending habits. She pushed for more openness and supervision, as well as audits and cost-cutting initiatives. Many member countries, particularly those suffering economic difficulties, agreed with this approach.

Security Council reform: Haley frequently criticized the UN Security Council's permanent membership, which has remained virtually unaltered since its creation. She called for the Council to be expanded to include developing countries and to provide greater regional representation, a view backed by many but opposed by current permanent members.

Human rights record: Haley cited the UN Human Rights Council as an example of hypocrisy since it includes nations with problematic human rights histories. She called for Council reform and increased scrutiny of its resolutions.

Strategies and Achievements

Haley's reform strategy was more than simply bluster. She used a variety of tactics, including:

- Her heated comments outlining the UN's failings drew media attention and popular support for reform, placing pressure on member nations to solve these concerns.

- **Strategic alliances:** To press for specific changes, Haley effectively formed coalitions with like-minded member states, particularly smaller nations disgruntled by the dominance of larger powers.

- **Withdrawal as a measure of leverage:** In a contentious move, Haley threatened to remove the United States from some United Nations groups, such as the Human Rights Council, if changes were not made. This technique produced mixed effects, resulting in some modest reforms but also hurting ties with allies who preferred a more collaborative approach.

Challenges and Reactions

Haley's reform attempts were not without difficulty:

- **Institutional inertia:** The United Nations' complicated bureaucracy and entrenched interests stymied development. Many improvements needed unanimity among member nations, a difficult process given the organization's various interests and past conflicts.

- friends opposed her combative methods and unilateral threats: Some of Haley's closest friends, such as European nations, preferred a more diplomatic approach to reform. This sowed discord within the Western bloc, impeding coordinated action.

- **Accusations of hypocrisy:** Critics questioned Haley's sincerity, pointing to the US's own human rights record and involvement in many wars. This hypocritical argument undercut her moral authority and efforts.

Standing with Israel

Nikki Haley's unwavering support for Israel marked her tenure as United States Ambassador to the United Nations. She became a staunch defender of the country on the international scene, defying criticism, campaigning for its security, and pressing for more international recognition. Her position established her reputation as a supporter of Israel in the United States, as well as her relationship with a critical geopolitical ally.

Her affection for Israel extends beyond political considerations. She established a personal connection to the nation and its cultural ideals while growing up in a Christian home with strong ties to the Jewish community.

Throughout her diplomatic career, this personal connection propelled her impassioned advocacy.

At the United Nations, Haley challenged Israel's critics square on. She condemned biased resolutions aimed at the country, blasted the Human Rights Council's anti-Israel agenda, and questioned the Palestinian narrative of the conflict. Her heated statements demonstrated her unwavering support for Israel's right to self-defence and validity as a nation.

Haley wasn't satisfied with simply defence. She vigorously supported worldwide recognition of Jerusalem as Israel's capital, contradicting US policy by shifting the American embassy there. She also advocated for Israel's inclusion in international organizations and supported diplomatic relations between Israel and other countries.

Challenges and Controversy

Haley's steadfast support for Israel elicited conflicting reactions:

Israel and supporters praised her as a sincere ally and staunch defender of their interests. Her outspoken support resonated with Israelis and pro-Israel organizations in the United States, strengthening her political image.

Palestinians and others accused her of prejudice, hampering peace efforts, and contributing to the perpetuation of the Israeli-Palestinian conflict. Her strong comments and seeming unwavering support for Israel aroused questions about her impartiality and the risk of worsening relations.

The international community is split in its view. Some supporters praised her candor and dedication to Israel's security, while others voiced concern about heightened polarization and the possibility of diplomatic gridlock.

Nikki Haley's stint as US Ambassador to the UN was defined by her unwavering support for Israel. Her activism focuses on two main areas: opposing anti-Israel resolutions and boosting Israel's worldwide recognition.

1. Objecting to Anti-Israel Resolutions:

Countering Narratives: Haley strongly opposed Israeli criticism. She fought back against narratives that portrayed Israel as an aggressor, emphasizing its right to self-defense and its complex security issues. Her talks frequently expressed opposing viewpoints, highlighting the flaws of the Palestinian Authority and Hamas' violent acts.

Beyond words, Haley used strategic voting techniques to prevent or weaken anti-Israel motions. She mobilized supporters, formed alliances, and used procedural procedures to affect results. Notably, she was instrumental in the rejection of multiple biased resolutions condemning Israeli settlements and unfairly criticizing Israel's conduct in response to Palestinian assaults.

Impact and Controversy: Israel and pro-Israel groups in the United States praised Haley's strategy for combating disinformation and protecting Israel's security interests. Critics, on the other hand, questioned her tactics, claiming that they inflamed the issue, hampered diplomatic attempts, and potentially jeopardized the UN's neutrality.

2. Promoting International Recognition of Israel:

The relocation of the US embassy to Jerusalem was Haley's most disruptive step, violating decades of US policy and recognizing the city as Israel's capital. This action conveyed a strong symbolic statement, enhancing

Israel's international position but infuriating Palestinians and many Arab countries.

Increasing Diplomatic Cooperation: Haley strongly urged other countries to follow suit and open embassies in Jerusalem. She also advocated for Israel's membership in international organizations such as UNESCO and encouraged bilateral diplomatic connections between Israel and other nations.

Consequences and complications: Haley's embassy relocation have mixed results. While it strengthened Israel's position in Jerusalem and raised morale among supporters, it also heightened tensions, hampered peace talks, and alienated Palestinians and crucial Arab allies. The long-term consequences of this diplomatic change are still being debated.

Controversy and Resignation

Nikki Haley's unexpected departure as US Ambassador to the United Nations in October 2018 ignited a media frenzy and left a swirling cloud of intrigue and controversy in her wake. Others assumed internal divisions and growing concerns with the Trump administration, while some saw it as a calculated move preparing the way for a presidential candidacy. Regardless of her motivations, her departure represented a watershed moment in her political career, leaving a complicated legacy of accomplishments, problems, and unanswered questions.

Many people were surprised by Haley's departure announcement, which she gave directly to President Trump in the Oval Office. Speculation abounds: Was it a premeditated effort to capitalize on her popularity and launch a presidential campaign? Did she have unspoken grievances with the administration's policy or internal disagreements with other officials? Her imprecise public pronouncements fueled the discussion while keeping everyone speculating about her next move.

Mixed Reactions and Unanswered Questions

Her resignation elicited a range of reactions:

Supporters: Highlighted her strong stance against enemies like Iran and her steadfast support for Israel, while applauding her UN successes. They regarded her departure as a chance for her to run for higher office, believing that her outspoken attitude and foreign policy knowledge would appeal to voters.

Critics: questioned her intentions, speculating that she resigned to avoid being linked to any scandals or because of internal conflicts within the government. They saw her departure as a sign of Trump's fractious inner circle and questioned the sincerity of her public apologies.

International Community: She expressed concerns about the impact of her departure on US foreign policy and the viability of the United Nations. Some feared a return to isolationism, while others hoped for a return to a more conciliatory attitude.

Haley's time at the UN was filled with both accomplishments and scandals. She rose to prominence as a formidable advocate for US interests, fighting rivals, defending Israel, and pressing for UN reform. Her combative methods, unshakable commitment to Trump, and withdrawal from important international accords such as the Paris Climate Accord, on the other hand, left a legacy of divisiveness and uncertainty.

Despite her return to the United States, Haley's political future remains uncertain. Whether she runs for president, returns to government service, or takes a different path, her time at the UN will throw a long shadow. Questions concerning her reasons for resignation, the exact amount of her influence inside the Trump administration, and the long-term consequences of her initiatives will be argued in the coming months.

The surprise departure of Nikita Haley as United States Ambassador to the United Nations in 2018 caused shockwaves through the political scene, prompting conjecture that swiftly consolidated into many main theories:

1. The Presidential Ambitions Theory: According to this widely held belief, Haley's departure was a deliberate maneuver to capitalize on her high profile and public popularity ratings, clearing the way for a possible presidential bid in 2020. This hypothesis was bolstered by media reports showing her increased popularity among Republican voters and her tight links to powerful funders. Her imprecise phrase about "exploring new horizons" fuelled this assumption even further.

2. Dissatisfaction and Internal Conflicts: Other hypotheses focus on internal conflict within the Trump administration. Rumors swirled that Haley was at odds with other officials, especially John Bolton, over foreign policy issues. Leaks indicated dissatisfaction with the administration's direction as well as a lack of control over critical choices. Her public comments suggested "different directions" for US foreign policy, providing credibility to the thesis of simmering disagreement.

3. The Strategic Escape Artist: Some regarded Haley's departure as a pre-emptive move to avoid being linked to any Trump administration problems or the expected aftermath from a Democratic triumph in 2020. By resigning early, she would be able to retain her favorable image and future opportunities regardless of the administration's destiny. Critics who saw her departure as a premeditated escape from a sinking ship agreed with this interpretation.

4. Personal Reasons and Burned Out: Some felt that, aside from political considerations, personal motivations played a role. Rumors of family issues and job-related exhaustion circulated. While such personal reasons are rarely openly stated, they cannot be completely discounted as causes for her decision.

Analyzing the Evidence

- Deciphering Haley's genuine motivations necessitates a thorough examination of various evidence:
- Examining publications, interviews, and leaks for insights into internal dynamics and Haley's own statements.
- Official statements: Investigating her resignation speech and subsequent public remarks for indications about her mental health and future goals.
- Weighing the viewpoints of seasoned political watchers and individuals with firsthand knowledge of the Trump administration.

While a conclusive conclusion may remain elusive, a thorough examination of the facts can provide light on the most likely narratives as well as the relative strength of each proposal.

PART 4

The Road to 2024

After Nikki Haley resigned from her position as US ambassador to the UN in 2018, there was a vacuum in the political scene that led to rumors regarding her aspirations going forward. As the drumbeat of the 2024 presidential election beat harder, Haley's name is regularly near the top of the list of probable Republican candidates. A successful campaign, on the other hand, will need traversing a complicated landscape of prior accomplishments, ongoing issues, and a large field of contenders.

Haley's journey to the White House begins with solidifying her base and forging new alliances. This entails:

Leveraging Strengths: Using her skills as a captivating speaker, a strong champion for American interests, and an experienced foreign policy specialist to her advantage. It will be critical to reach out to key segments, notably women and minorities.

Fundraising Prowess: In today's political atmosphere, demonstrating financial prowess is critical. Cultivating ties with contributors, both within and beyond the Republican Party, will be a vital early goal.

Putting Together a Team: To negotiate the convoluted maze of the campaign trail, she will need to surround herself with seasoned campaign advisers, knowledgeable strategists, and dedicated operatives.

Reconciliation with the Past: Haley's relationship with the Trump administration is a two-edged sword. While his followers may see her ties as an advantage, others who have qualms about Trump's legacy may be hesitant to support her campaign. This calls for:

Maintaining Distance: Maintaining distance from some of Trump's most divisive ideas and views while recognizing his achievements and promoting common Republican principles will be a tricky balancing act.

Carving a Unique Identity: Haley must distinguish herself from other possible candidates by projecting a distinct vision and policy agenda that connects with voters while being respectable inside the Republican fold.

Addressing critiques: To address possible concerns among independent voters and moderate Republicans, she will need to openly address critiques of her prior beliefs and actions, particularly on subjects such as immigration and climate change.

Getting a Glimpse of the Competition

The field of possible Republican contenders is expected to be large, with each candidate having their own set of strengths and flaws. Haley's approach will include the following steps:

Messaging and Differentiation: Carefully developing a message that distinguishes her from the competition, emphasizing her unique experiences and qualifications while addressing the major issues of swing voters.

Early Primary States: Concentrating attention on early primary states like as Iowa and New Hampshire, where she hopes to create strong grassroots support and momentum that will carry her candidacy ahead.

Building Coalitions: The ability to appeal to different wings of the Republican Party, including moderates and conservatives, will be critical in gaining the nomination.

Running as a Republican

Nikki Haley's probable run for the White House isn't a one-woman show. She enters a crowded battlefield, a Republican primary field brimming with established personalities and eager newcomers. Here, she confronts the simultaneous task of carving out a distinct route among the crowds while also articulating a message that connects with voters and sets her apart from the pack.

The Republican field is filled with a wide range of candidates, each with their own set of strengths and shortcomings. Haley is required to:

Identify prospective Allies and Opponents: Recognizing prospective strategic partners and rivals for voter attention is critical. Building bridges while maintaining her own individuality will be a tough balancing act.

Use her Differentiators: Haley's foreign policy competence and personality are evident assets. Using her unique experiences and presenting a bold, new voice can help her stand out as a viable choice.

Positioning oneself strategically will impact her messaging and target audience, depending on whether she caters to moderates or appeals to the base. The capacity to strike a balance between ideological purity and electability will be critical.

Creating her Platform

Aside from name recognition, people want substance. Haley's platform must include:

Key Domestic Issues: Addressing issues like as inflation, healthcare, and education reform with specific measures that address citizens' everyday problems.

Foreign Policy Vision: Defining America's role in the world, addressing concerns like as China, Russia, and global security challenges.

A Unifying Message: Weaving a story that transcends Republican Party disagreements and appeals to a broader demographic, maybe by concentrating on shared topics like as economic opportunity and national security.

Opportunities and Challenges

Creating a winning platform among varied views takes considerable thought:

Finding the Sweet Spot: To appeal to the Republican base while also recruiting independent votes or moderate Republicans, policy positions and language must be carefully calibrated.

Avoiding Me-Tooism entails providing her own nuanced ideas and unique solutions in order to distinguish herself from other candidates with similar stances.

Accepting Unforeseen Issues: The political scene is ever-changing. Haley must be agile in order to adapt to developing difficulties and solve unanticipated obstacles.

The Search for Resonance

Finally, success is dependent on engaging with voters:

Authenticity and charisma: Projecting honesty and true love for her platform will appeal to viewers looking for genuine dedication.

Effective Communication: Mastering the art of clear, succinct communication in stump speeches and media appearances is critical for catching attention and effectively communicating her message.

A Sprinkling of Audacity: Standing out necessitates taking calculated risks with unique policy suggestions or courageous stands on crucial subjects.

The Road Ahead

Navigating the crowded Republican field and developing a convincing program are only the beginning of Haley's future presidential campaign. Future chapters might go into further detail about:

- **Specific Policy Positions:** Analyzing Haley's views on major topics like as immigration, abortion, gun control, and climate change, as well as the implications for her candidacy.

- Examining Haley's performance in debates and public appearances, as well as her strengths and flaws in presenting her message to a national audience.
- Exploring Haley's plan for communicating with voters at the local level, generating support in critical states, and organizing volunteers and campaign operatives.
- Analyzing Haley's strategy to communicating with the media, leveraging social media platforms, and navigating the sometimes-tumultuous waters of press coverage.

Priorities and policy positions

Nikki Haley's future campaign is dependent not just on personality and strategy, but also on the specific positions she takes on the subjects that are most important to voters. Understanding her policy ideas and goals is critical for determining her potential popularity and the course she would pursue if elected.

Foreign Policy

Haley's strength rests in international policy, where she is expected to be forceful and assertive:

Countering China: Expect a sustained emphasis on China as a key strategic adversary, advocating for a robust military presence in the Indo-Pacific and countering its economic and technical threats.

Russia and the Global Order: There will be a renewed emphasis on preserving the rules-based international order, which will most likely include a hard stance against Russian aggression and boosting American leadership in global institutions.

Middle East Engagement: While remaining supportive of Israel, Haley may strive to rebalance US participation in the area, emphasizing diplomatic solutions and minimizing military commitment.

Domestic Concerns

Domestically, Haley's positions paint a more complicated picture:

Economy and Trade: While likely backing tax cuts and deregulation, Haley may take a more nuanced approach to trade accords and address income disparity issues.

Healthcare and Social Programs: Her positions on healthcare reform and social programs are unknown, however she may favor a conservative approach centered on personal responsibility and market-based solutions.

Education and the Environment: Expect an emphasis on school choice and promoting American ideals in education, but her position on environmental laws remains unclear, with her perhaps calling for a balance between economic growth and environmental protection.

Unknowns and Possible Surprisers

Several difficulties provide opportunity for Haley to stand out:

Gun Control: Given her track record as governor of South Carolina, she may push for gun rights while supporting more moderate measures such as background checks.

Immigration: A significant pillar in her campaign might be striking a compromise between border security and a road to citizenship for unauthorized immigrants.

Social Issues: Haley's beliefs on abortion, same-sex marriage, and other social issues are hazy, leaving room for her to alter her ideas to appeal to various voter categories.

Challenges and Controversy

Nikki Haley's future presidential run promises to be an exciting but tumultuous ride. While her charm, foreign policy skills, and bold ideas fascinate audiences, she also faces a challenging and contentious environment. Scrutiny looms, and she will need to overcome enormous difficulties if she is to win. Let's look at the various hurdles she could face and the techniques she could use to overcome them.

One of Haley's most difficult difficulties arises from her strong relationship with the Trump administration. While some see this as a benefit, others are concerned about the possible consequences:

Trump's Shadow: She will have to walk a fine line between acknowledging Trump's successes and keeping Republican support.

Personal criticisms: Previous words and actions on matters like as immigration and climate change may reemerge, necessitating clear explanations and maybe amended viewpoints to meet concerns.

Perception of Loyalty: Her steadfast devotion to Trump may be seen by detractors as an indication of blind adherence, casting doubt on her capacity for autonomous judgment.

Navigating the Political Terrain

Aside from Trump, Haley's path is fraught with possible stumbling blocks:

Crowded Field: The Republican primary promises to be very contested, with both seasoned and emerging contenders fighting for the nomination. Haley must set herself apart by bold statements, clever partnerships, and a captivating narrative.

Fundraising Frenzy: Obtaining appropriate financial support is critical for campaign success. Convincing funders to support her agenda while competing with well-established fundraising engines will be a major task.

Media Scrutiny: Every facet of her campaign, from policy ideas to personal choices, will be closely scrutinized by the media. Maintaining composure, communicating clearly, and successfully responding to criticism will be critical.

Overcoming Difficulties

Overcoming these obstacles necessitates smart manoeuvring and resilience:

Embracing Transparency: Addressing previous criticisms and concerns openly, even with subtle clarifications or even amended perspectives, helps disarm prospective assaults and display a commitment to learn and adapt.

Making a Mark: Emphasizing her unique experiences, foreign policy skills, and new viewpoint can help her build a place in a crowded industry.

Building Strong Connections with Local Communities, Engaging Volunteers, and Effectively Using Campaign Resources will be critical for obtaining critical votes in important states.

Using Media Platforms: Mastering the art of clear and succinct communication through traditional media and social media is critical to catching attention, successfully communicating her message, and connecting with voters.

PART 5

Personal Life and Reflections

On September 7, 1996, Faith Haley married Michael Haley. They held both Sikh and Methodist rituals to commemorate the occasion. Rena and Nalin are the couple's two children.

Haley became a Christian in 1997. Her husband and she are regulars at the United Methodist Church. She also goes to Sikh services maybe one or twice a year. During a trip to India in 2014, she took her spouse to the Harmandir Sahib. When asked if she hopes her parents convert to Christianity during a Christianity Today interview, Haley replied, *"What I hope is that my parents do what's right for them."*

Her spouse, a South Carolina Army National Guard officer, served in Afghanistan in 2013. Haley and her family live on Kiawah Island in South Carolina, near Charleston.

In 2019, Haley's net worth was estimated to be $1 million. Her net worth is expected to reach $8 million by 2022, thanks in part to book sales and appointments to the boards of directors of Boeing and United Homes Group. Balancing rigorous public service with wife and parenting obligations has been a continual struggle, requiring a balancing act of allocating time and sustaining relationships. Haley's Sikh faith is also important in forming her moral compass and giving her with strength and guidance. It is a part of her life, not just a title she wears.

Haley has encountered hardship as a woman of Indian ancestry negotiating a primarily white and male political milieu. Her path has been distinguished by perseverance and the drive to smash glass ceilings, from fighting subtle prejudices to suffering overt sexist statements. Her experiences have given her a unique perspective on societal injustices and fueled her enthusiasm for campaigning for tolerance and diversity.

Beyond politics, Haley's commitment to helping people is evident in her charity efforts. She actively attempts to make a good influence on society, from supporting literacy programs and healthcare efforts to promoting the empowerment of women and girls. These activities reflect a profound sense of compassion and a genuine desire to make the world a better place for everybody.

Despite future uncertainty, Haley's dedication to public service is unshakeable. Whether she pursues another political chapter, writes a book, or devotes herself to charity pursuits, one thing is certain: her voice and impact will not disappear. She represents a new generation of leaders, one motivated by ambition, purpose, and a desire to leave a lasting legacy.

Timeline of Key Events and Milestones in Nikki Haley's Life

- **1972:** Born Nimrata Randhawa in Bamberg, South Carolina, to Sikh immigrants from Punjab, India.
- **1994:** Graduates from Clemson University with a Bachelor of Science in accounting.
- **1996:** Marries Michael Haley, a veteran and entrepreneur.
- **2003:** Joins the Orangeburg County Chamber of Commerce Board of Directors.

- **2004:** Elected Treasurer of the National Association of Women Business Owners.
- **2005:** Elected to the South Carolina House of Representatives, becoming the first Indian-American to hold this position in the state.
- **2008:** Re-elected to the South Carolina House of Representatives.
- **2010:** Elected Governor of South Carolina, becoming the first female and person of color to hold this office in the state.
- **2011-2017:** Serves two terms as Governor of South Carolina, focusing on economic development, education reform, and infrastructure improvements.
- **2016:** Campaigns for Marco Rubio in the Republican presidential primary.
- **2017:** Appointed U.S. Ambassador to the United Nations by President Donald Trump.
- **2018:** Resigns as U.S. Ambassador to the United Nations.
- **2019:** Establishes Stand for America, a policy group promoting public policies focused on strengthening the economy, culture, and national security.
- **2020:** Joins the board of directors of Boeing.

- **2021:** Becomes a lifetime member of the Clemson University Board of Trustees.
- **2023:** Begins campaigning for the 2024 Republican presidential nomination.
- **2024:** Potential election as the first female and person of color to become President of the United States (pending the outcome of the election).

Noteworthy Milestones

- First non-European American and first female governor of South Carolina.
- Second Indian American governor to be elected in the United States.
- Youngest woman to serve as governor of South Carolina.
- First female U.S. Ambassador to the United Nations from South Carolina.
- Potential first female and first person of color to be elected President of the United States.

CONCLUSION

The final brushstroke falls, and Nikki Haley's portrait stands before us, not a static image, but a kaleidoscope pulsating with possibility. We've seen the fire in her eyes, the steel in her spine, the tapestry of her path stitched with family, faith, and an unstoppable ambition.

This is not the conclusion of her narrative, but rather a pregnant pause, a breath before the following stanza. Will she rise to the highest position, breaking another glass barrier with a sari and a smile? Will she choose a different route, leaving her mark in unexpected places throughout the world? Only the winds of fate are aware.

But one thing is certain: Nikki Haley is not a bystander on life's stage. She's a filmmaker, creating her own story, defying expectations, and pushing a generation to think beyond their neighborhoods. She murmurs in a Southern belle's voice, but roars with the determination of a lioness guarding her pride.

Her journey is a monument to the human spirit, and it serves as a light of hope for those who dare to go against the stream. It serves as a reminder that success is a dance on a tightrope, a constant balancing of ambition and compassion, strength and vulnerability.

So, let us remember Nikki Haley for the fire that burns inside her, the tapestry she continues to weave, and the message she whispers to the world: your ambitions, no matter how daring, are worth pursuing.

In the end, her legacy will be measured not by marble monuments or Oval Office portraits, but by the hearts she ignited, the voices she amplified, and the unwavering belief she instilled in all of us: that the kaleidoscope of our lives, with all of its vibrant contradictions and shifting patterns, is a masterpiece in the making.

So, go on and create your own masterpiece. Allow Nikki Haley's tale to be your brushstroke, your inspiration, your reminder that we are all artists in the big fabric of life, capable of constructing narratives that resonate throughout generations.

This is not the end of the story. It's a fresh start. And everything is conceivable on this blank canvas.

9 798876 165497